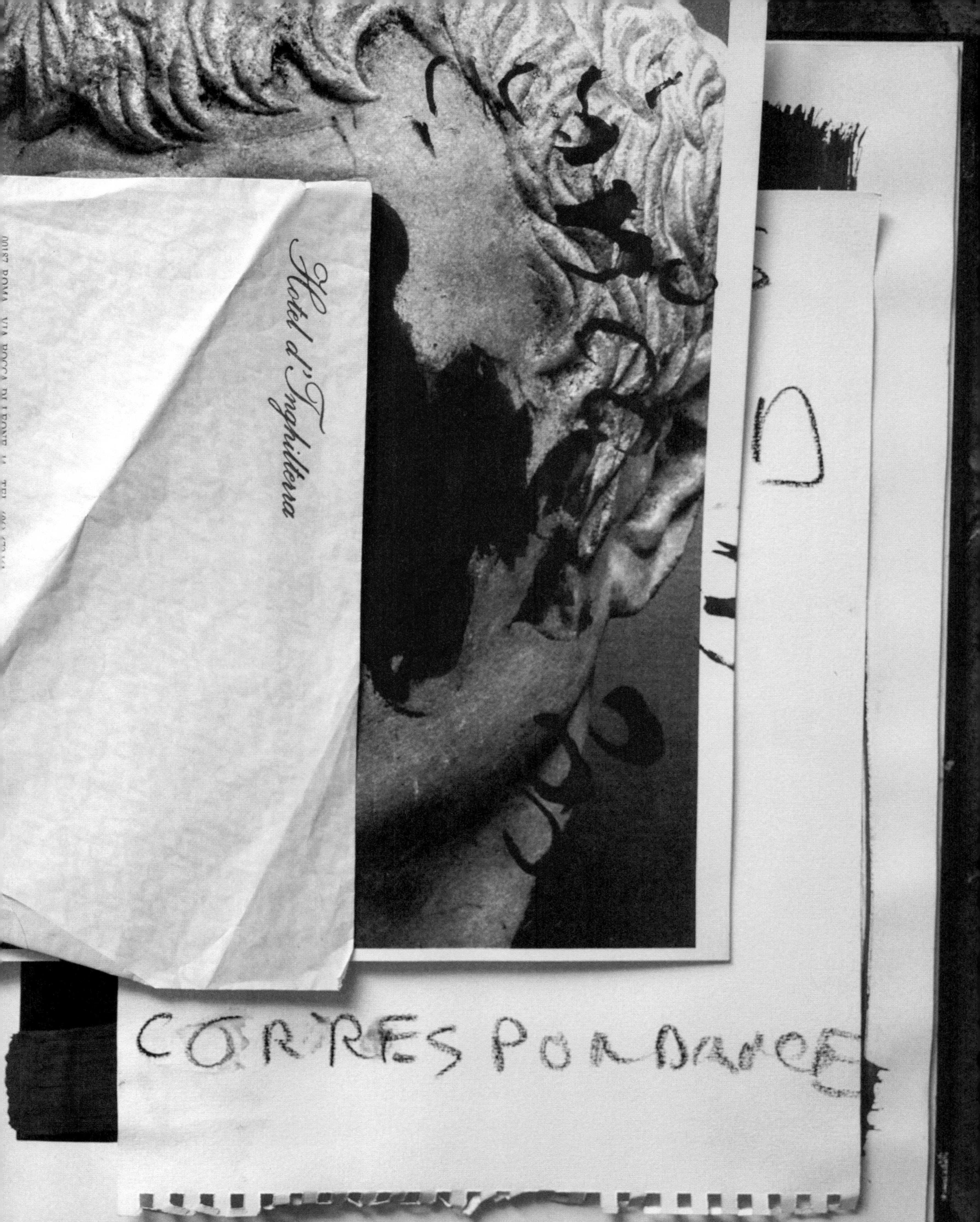

Hotel d'Inghilterra

CORRESPONDANCE

Encyclopedie +

luigi ghini

Magazine .

+ (Punto della

dogana)   Venise !

Portrait +

Ettore Sottsas

cahier de l'evenement

villa Palagonia

la malcon

+ cahier on

styn sculptu

villa Palada

cotage / a

Venise .

Visite Priées. ⊗

DOLCE GABANNA

ITALY ⟶ ✳

+ ✓ MC ALBINE ⟶ ✳
+ ✳ Malaparte
    Mona Williams
+ ✳ dolfino
+ ✳ V. Medici ✳
+ ✳ Panza di Buimo ✳
+ ✳ BOMARZO. ✳
* BRANDOLINI ~
+ ✳ Karl in Rome
⊕ ~ Valentino ✳ Punto della
                    dogana
+ ✕ SCRAP Book Venice
+ BIENALE DE VENISE.

Agnelli "N   Vedla in ITALY"
Vedla   COURT Thecla in ITALY"

ANNA WINTOUR

LA CONSOLATION DE L'ABSENCE

PAR W DE L'AUNAY

—◻ it will be a sort
of collage, a kind of
scrap Book with photos

of different sizes esc:

villa malaparte :: 2 views by 3me
ou jo barraït de la maison [for the Mollivott
de carlo Mollino— or French
Print of Bomarzo gardens.
by "Carnet de Voyage"

Don FLAVIN

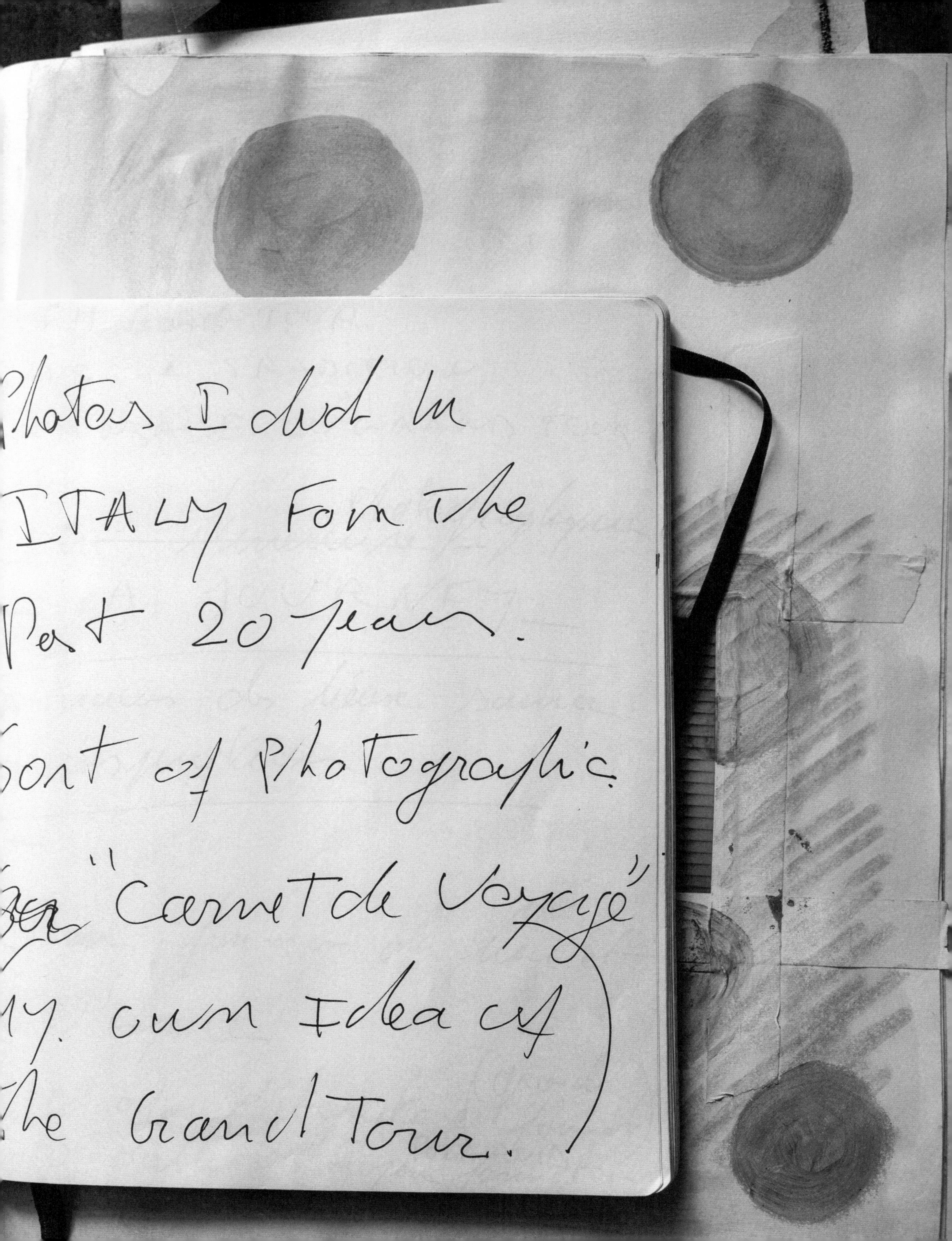

Photos I shot in
ITALY For the
Past 20 years.

sort of Photographic
"Carnet de Voyage"
My. own idea of
the Grand Tour.

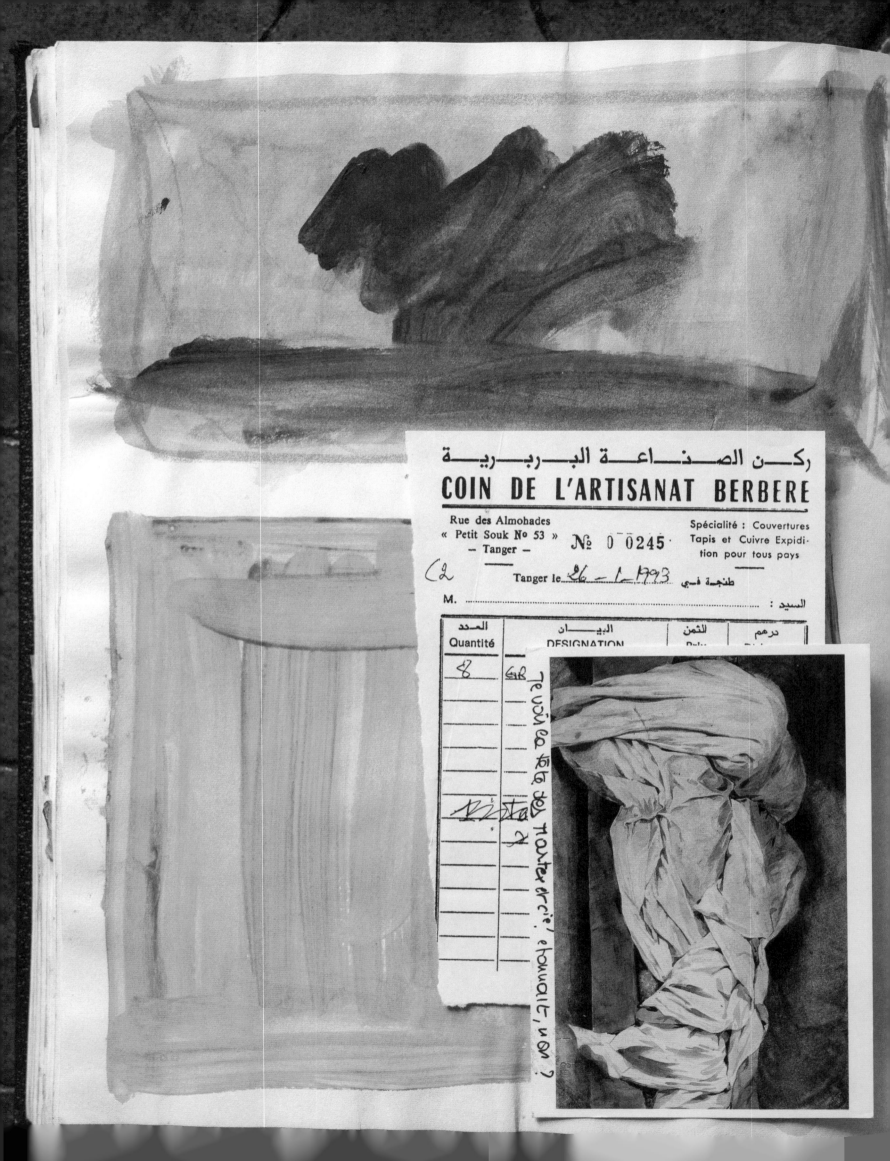

ركن الصناعة البربرية

COIN DE L'ARTISANAT BERBERE

Rue des Almohades
« Petit Souk N° 53 »
— Tanger —

Nº 0 0245

Spécialité : Couvertures
Tapis et Cuivre Expidi-
tion pour tous pays

Tanger le 26 - 1 - 1993   طنجة في

M. .... : السيد

العدد Quantité	البيــان DESIGNATION	الثمن Prix	درهم
8			

grafica Francesco Armitti / Sollimene – Giovanni Francesco Venturini, Loggia de la Villa Medicis (detail) d'après Le Fontane de' Palazzi e ne' Giardini di Roma, Rome, G.G. de Rossi, s.d.

FRANÇOIS HALARD

②

FRANÇOIS HALARD ②

A VISUAL DIARY

RIZZOLI
NEW YORK

New York · Paris · London · Milan

CONCEPT AND
EDITING BY
BEDA ACHERMANN

PERSONAL NOTES
BY
FRANÇOIS HALARD

PERSONAL NOTES

LUIS
BARRAGÁN
MEXICO
2018
POLAROIDS

CUADRA SAN CRISTÓBAL & CASA GILARDI

LOUISE BOURGEOIS

NEW YORK 2014

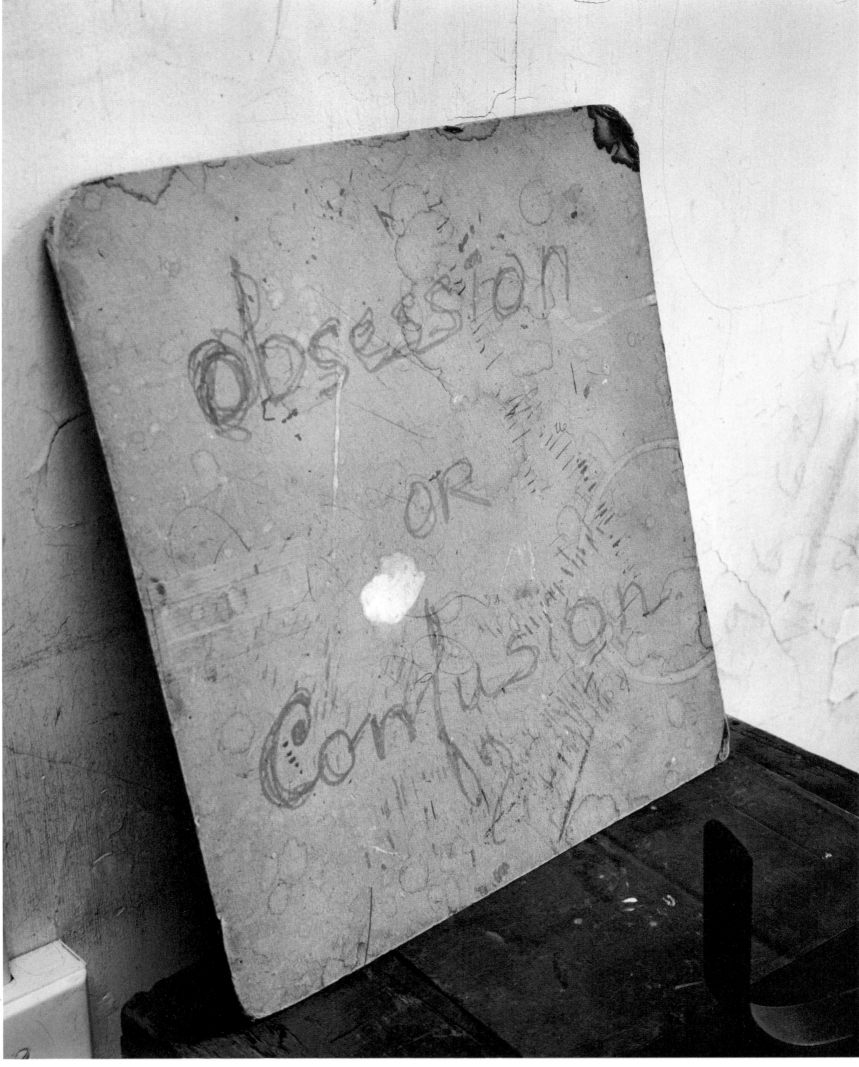

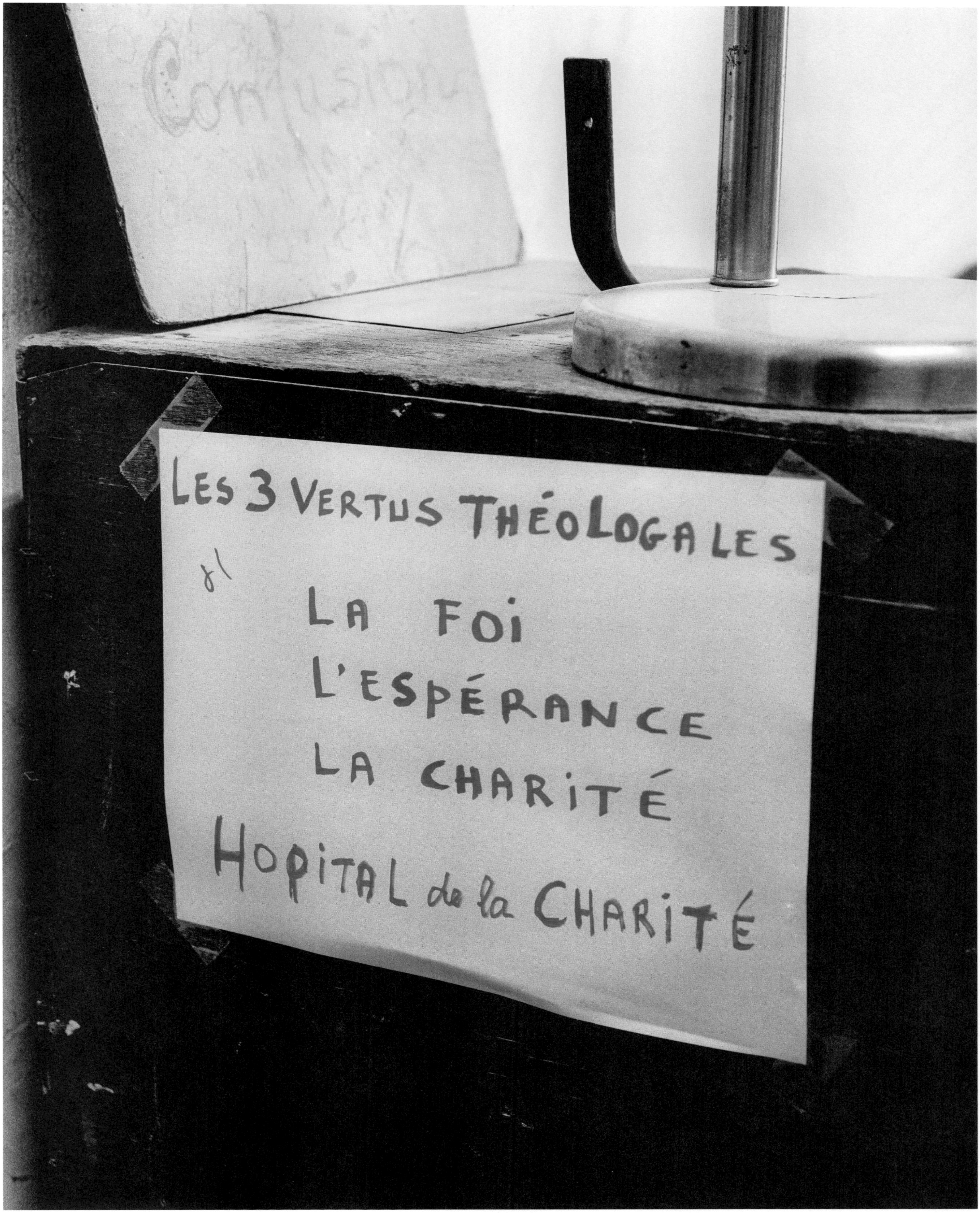
LES 3 VERTUS THÉOLOGALES
LA FOI
L'ESPÉRANCE
LA CHARITÉ
HOPITAL de la CHARITÉ

LOUISE'S KITCHEN

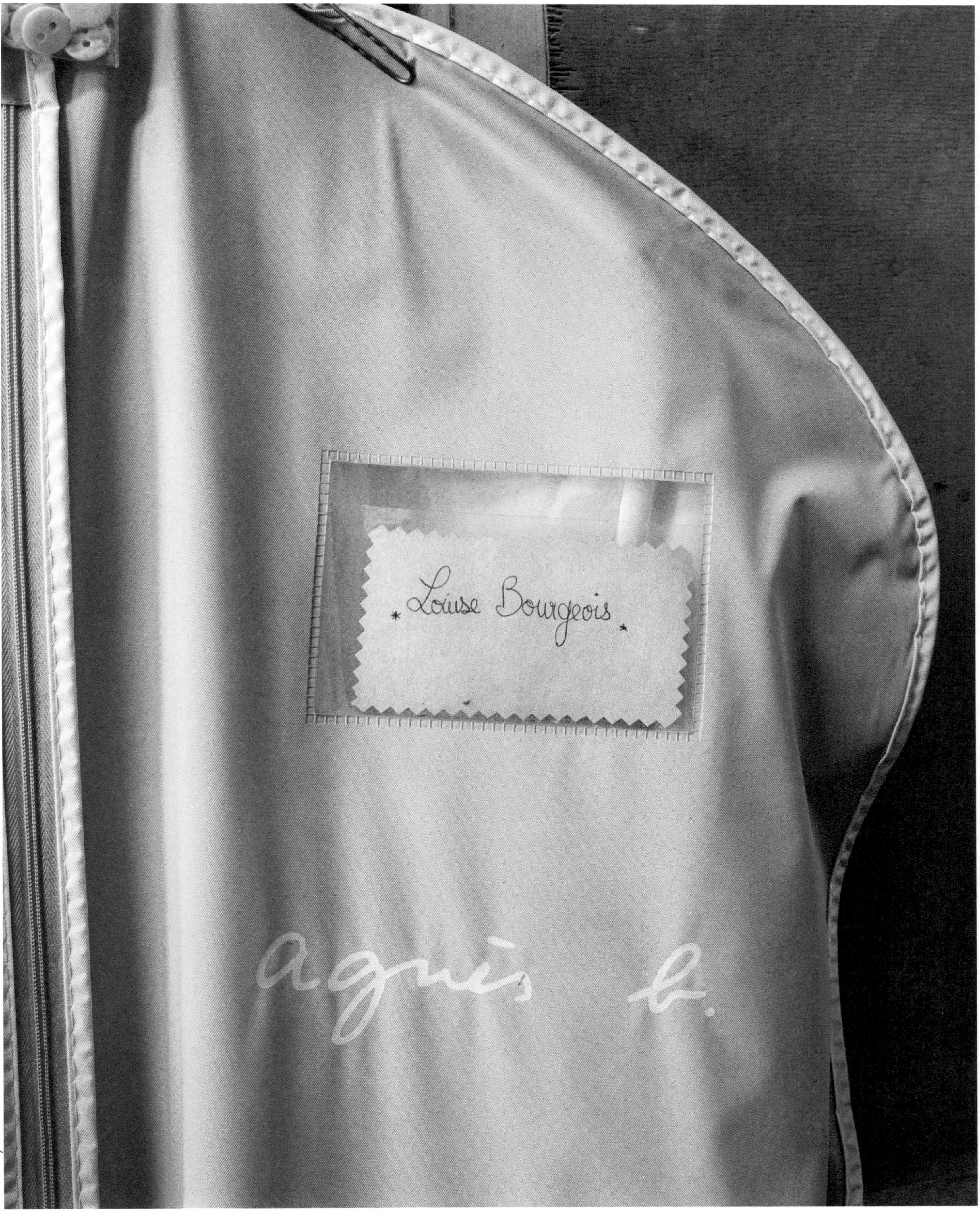

COURTESY THE EASTON FOUNDATION

1973

387

R246

Women Artists

1990 Engagement Book / Calendar

ON THE WALL BONO, DAMIEN HIRST
AND JERRY WITH LOUISE

LOUISE'S WALL

DOMINIQUE
DE MENIL'S

HOUSE
+
TEXAS
+
HOUSTON
+
PHILIP JOHNSON
+
CHARLES JAMES

2016

INTERIORS BY CHARLES JAMES
ARCHITECTURE BY PHILIP JOHNSON

PAINTING BY FERNAND LÉGER:
LA GRANDE PARADE

IN THE BEDROOM.   PAINTING BY CHRISTIAN BÉRARD

CHARLES JAMES SOFA

PORTRAITS OF JERMAYNE MACAGY
BY ANDY WARHOL

PAINTING BY KENNETH NOLAND

THE FORMER DOMINIQUE DE MENIL'S BEDROOM

PAINTING BY MAGRITTE

SOFA DESIGN BY CHARLES JAMES

PAINTING BY LUIS FERNÁNDEZ

MIQUEL
BARCELÓ
- PARIS
2018

PORTRAITS OF MIQUEL BY ANDY WARHOL

THE HOUSE

THE STUDIO

BOOKSHELVES BY ETTORE SOTTSASS

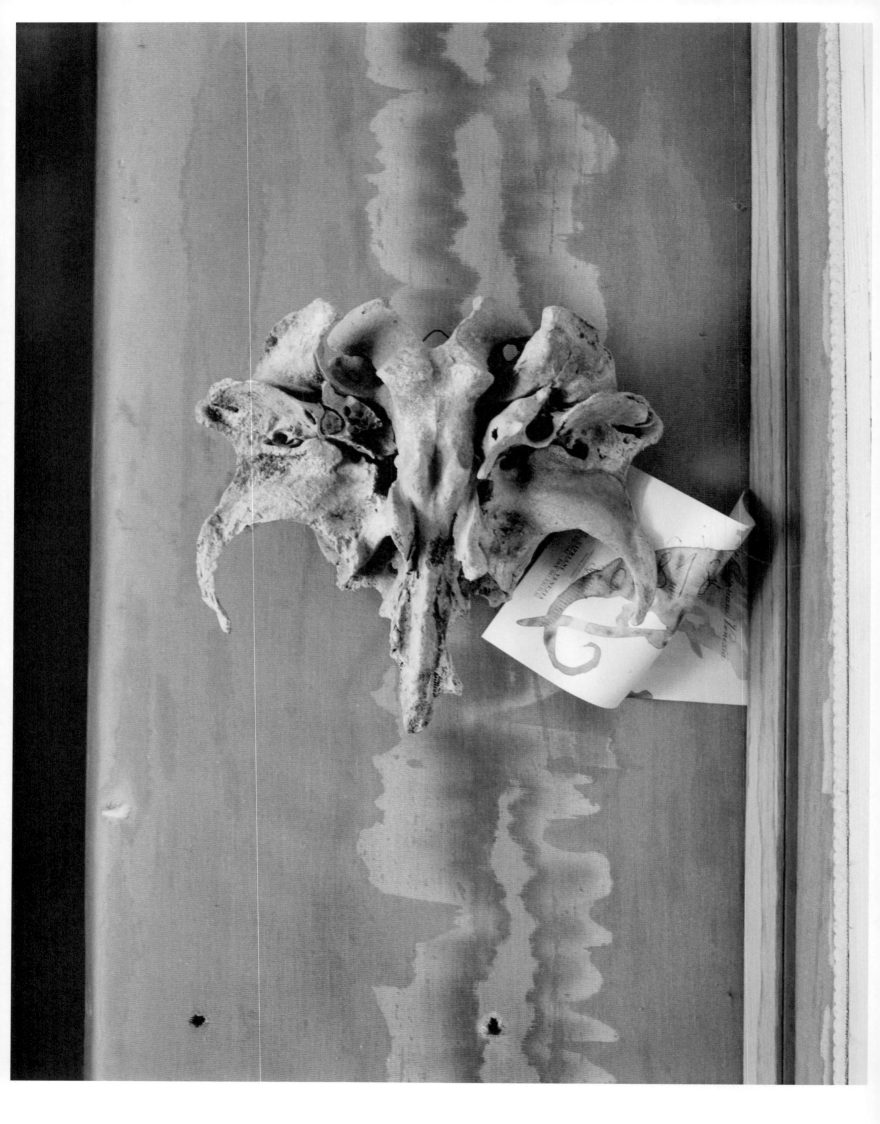

PAINTING BY MIKE BIDLO

SAMEDI 2 ET DIMANCHE 3 AV

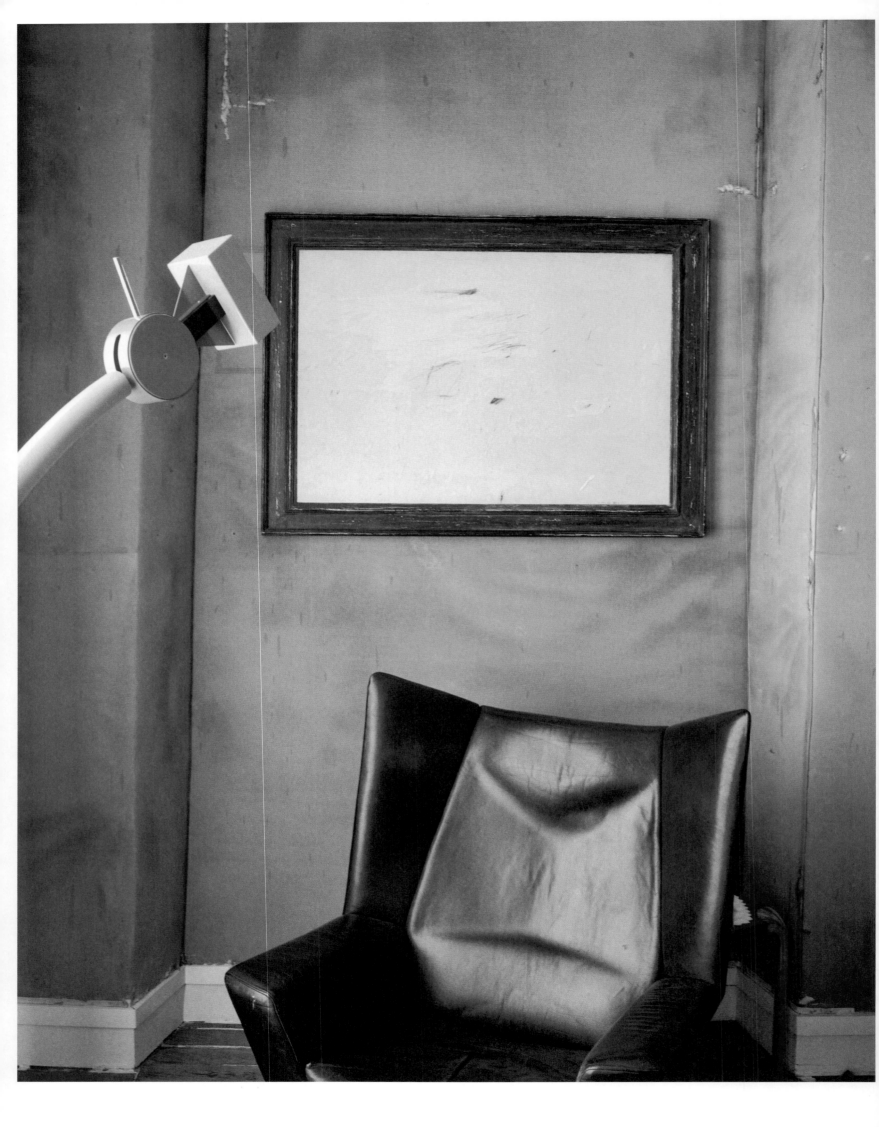

THE ATELIER DOWNSTAIRS

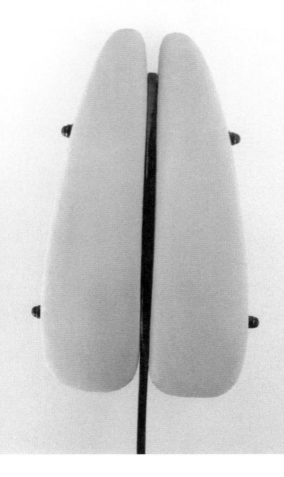

IN THE STAIRCASE MIQUEL BARCELÓ'S
BRONZE SCULPTURE L'ALLUMETTE

ANTONY
GORMLEY
HIGH
HOUSE
STUDIO
NORFOLK
2018

ANTONY GORMLEY AND VICKEN PARSONS'S
18TH-CENTURY VILLA

A HOWARD HODGKIN PRINT IN THE STAIRCASE

GORMLEY'S SMALL GUT FROM 2014

THE VILLA

THE STUDIO

GORMLEY AT WORK

DRIES'S

GARDEN &

FLOWERS

DRIES VAN NOTEN
PATRICK VANGHELUWE
VOGUE - BELGIUM - 2013

RAPHAEL
ROME

- VATICAN - VILLA MADAMA -
- VILLA FARNESINA - 2015

VILLA FARNESINA

CEILING IN THE VILLA MADAMA

RAPHAEL'S LOGGIA IN THE APOSTOLIC
PALACE AT THE VATICAN

RAPHAEL'S LOGGIA FOR THE POPE

CEILING IN THE VILLA FARNESINA

THE VILLA FARNESINA

RICK

OWENS

+

MICHÈLE LAMY

PARIS 2013

A SCULPTURE BY HORST-EGON KALINOWSKI
IN THE MEETING ROOM

ANTIQUE URN BY GEORGES HOENTSCHEL
WALL FRESCO BY SCARLETT ROUGE

PORTRAIT OF MICHÈLE LAMY BY STEVEN KLEIN

RICK OWENS'S STUDIO

RICK OWENS's BATHROOM

UFO

RONDINONE

2018

HARLEM, NEW YORK

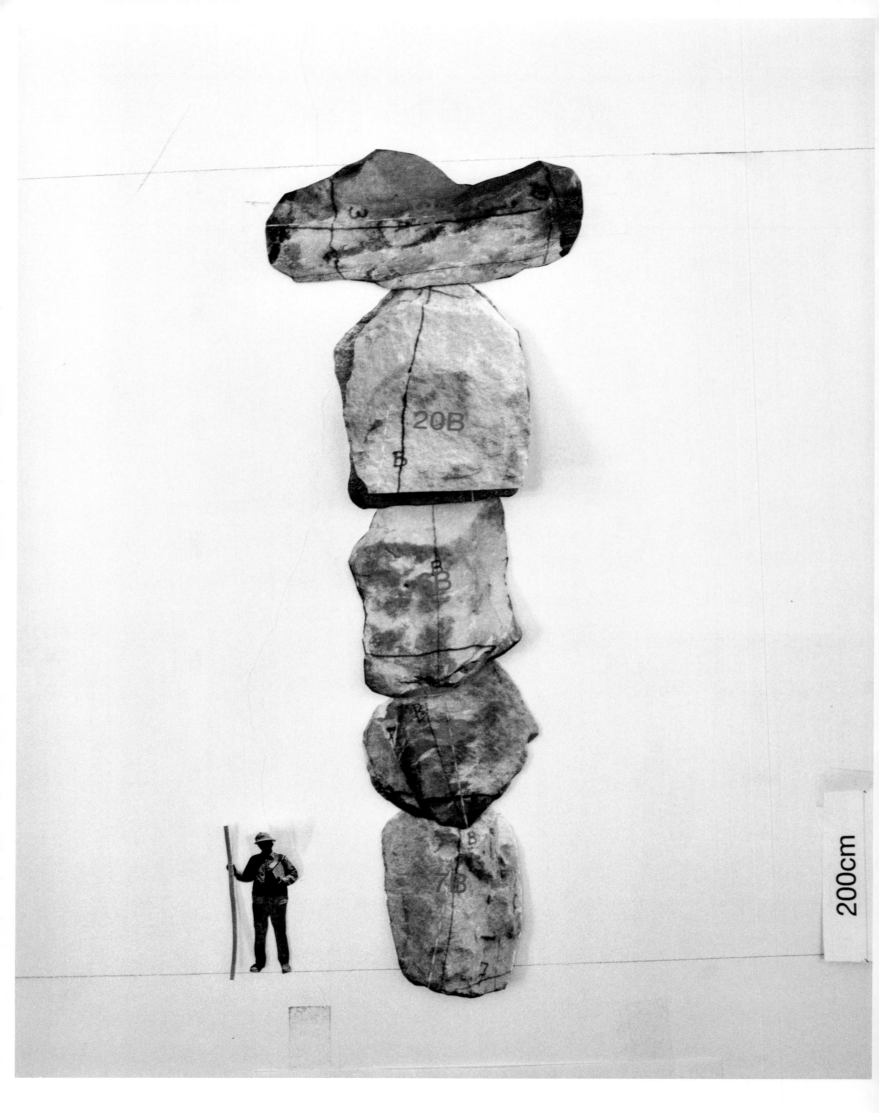

UGO RONDINONE   SCULPTURE MAQUETTE

ANDRES
SERRANO
NYC 2016

ANDRES SERRANO AND
IRINA MOVMYGA'S APARTMENT IN MANHATTAN

A PHOTOGRAPH BY E. J. BELLOCQ

PHOTO BY BARON VON GLOEDEN

ELEOUSA

RHODES

GREECE
2014

ITALIAN

ARCHITECTURE

THE VILLAGE OF ELEOUSA IN RHODES

FOUNDED BY ITALIANS IN 1935

JOHN
RICHARDSON

NEW YORK
5TH AVE

20017

PORTRAIT OF JOHN RICHARDSON BY ANDY WARHOL

PAINTING BY JULIAN SCHNABEL
YELLOW HEAD PORTRAIT BY GLORIA VON THURN UND TAXIS

WORKS BY PABLO PICASSO

JOHN'S PORTRAIT BY LUCIAN FREUD

LOULOU DE LA FALAISE BY JP MASCLET

PICASSO'S PORTRAIT BY VALENTINE HUGO

PICASSO·COCTEAU·DOUGLAS COOPER   BY DAVID DOUGLAS DUNCAN
IN THE STREETS OF ARLES

CAT DRAWING BY HUGO GUINNESS

PAINTING BY HARRIET LASSALLE

LUCIAN FREUD PAINTING THE QUEEN
PHOTOGRAPHED BY DAVID DAWSON IN 2001

GEORGES BRAQUE

MARC JACOBS

JOHN CURRIN

ELIZABETH PEYTON

PEACH BY ED RUSCHA

JACKIE BY ANDY WARHOL

GIACOMETTI AND BRAQUE

ED RUSCHA

GIACOMETTI

JEFF KOONS PUPPY

PAINTING BY GEORGE CONDO

RICHARD PRINCE

DAMIEN HIRST

JOHN CURRIN

EAVEN

ELIZABETH PEYTON

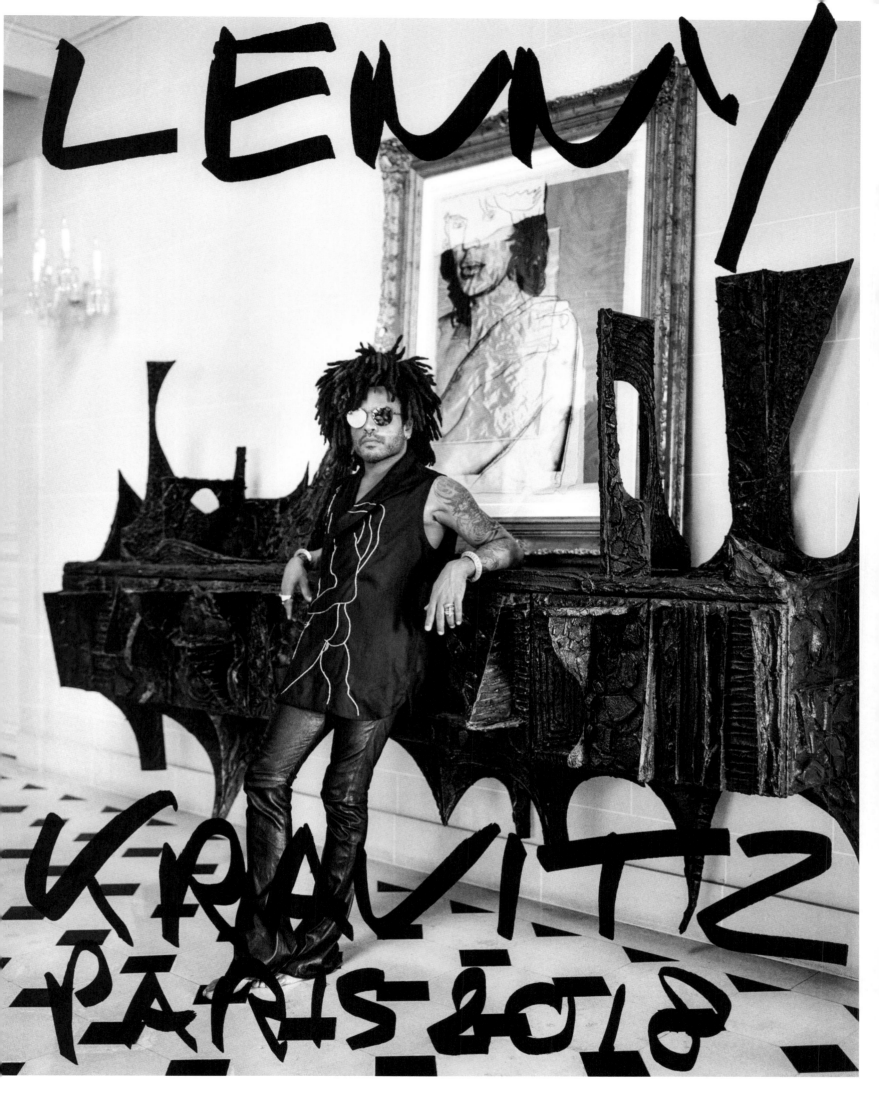

LENNY
KRAVITZ
PARIS 2018

PRINCE'S GUITAR AND SHOES

JOHN LENNON'S PORTRAIT
BY RICHARD AVEDON

MUHAMMAD ALI'S SHOES

LENNY AND HIS FATHER

MICK JAGGER BY ANDY WARHOL

MARILYN MONROE BY RICHARD AVEDON

LENNY AND HIS MOTHER

JAMES BROWN

MÉRIDA MEXICO 2015

IN THE STUDIO

IN THE BEDROOM

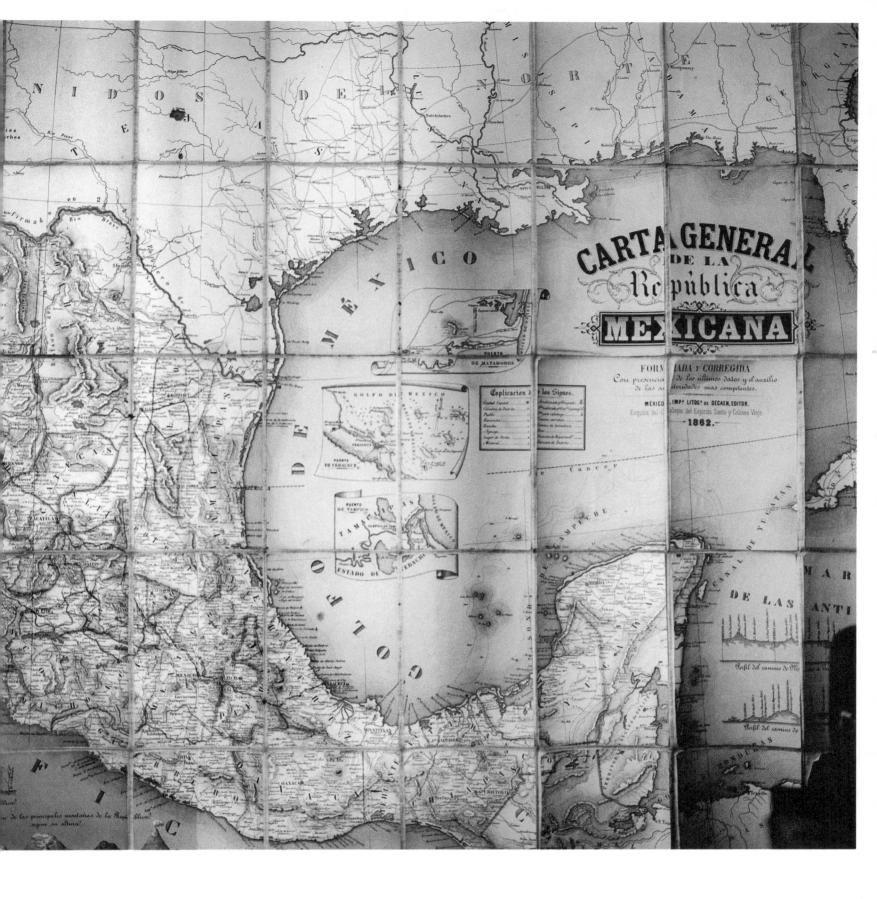

YUCATÁN

STUDIO

MARCANTE-TESTA

MILANO 2018

SAUL
LETTER
NEW
YORK
PHOTOGRAPHER

SAUL PORTRAIT AT THE SAUL LEITER FOUNDATION

2017

THE OLD STUDIO ON 10TH STREET IN NEW YORK

MARFA

CHINATI FOUNDATION

2005

MARFA TEXAS

CLAES OLDENBURG + COOSJE VAN BRUGGEN

DONALD JUDD

DAN FLAVIN

DAN FLAVIN

DONALD JUDD

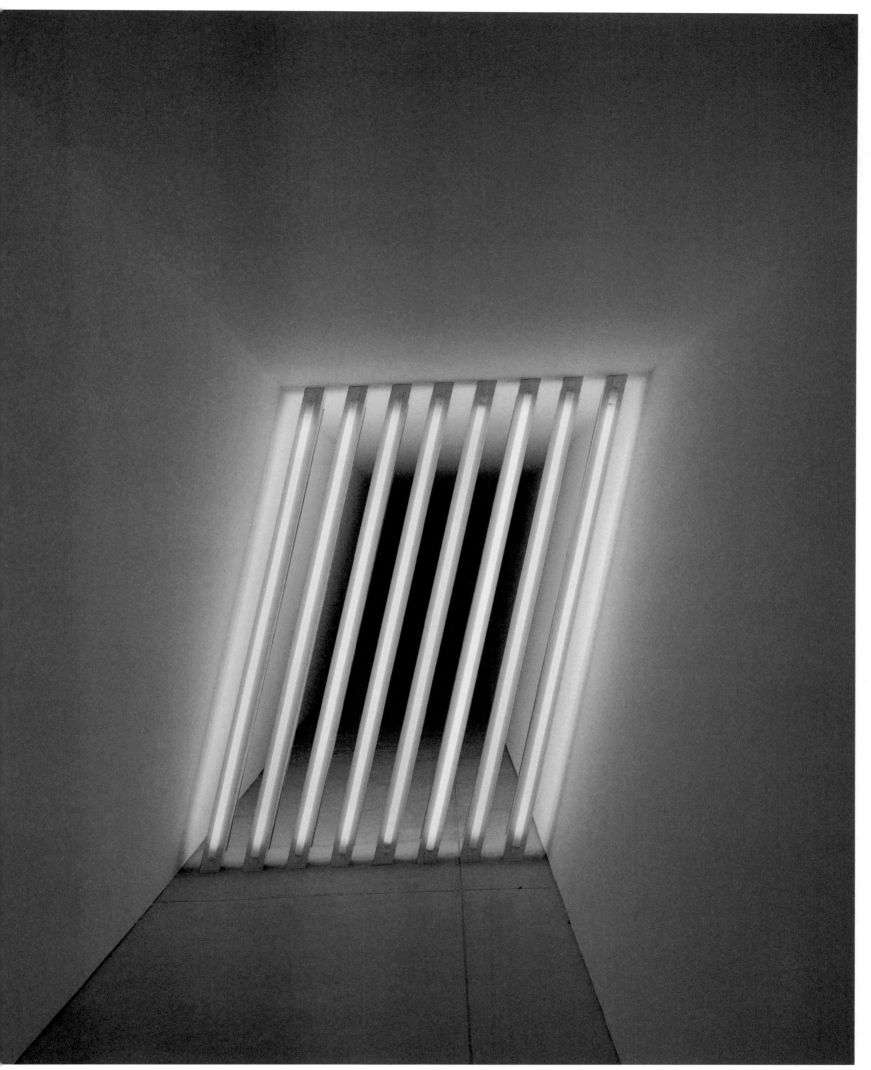

DAN FLAVIN

CHRIS GOSNEY AT LIZ LAMBERT RANCH IN TEXAS

EILEEN GRAY

VILLA E-1027

CAP
MODERNE
2018

IN THE BEDROOM

Ile Longue
de Clarence
Bahama
des Iles Ragged
Confites
Nuevitas del Principe
Manati
Padre
Gibara
Mge d'Alfred
Inagua
des Gonaïves
B. St Marc
Beaux Cayes
Maria
Annatto
Manchioneal

LE CORBUSIER PAINTED THIS MURAL WITHOUT
EILEEN GRAY'S APPROVAL

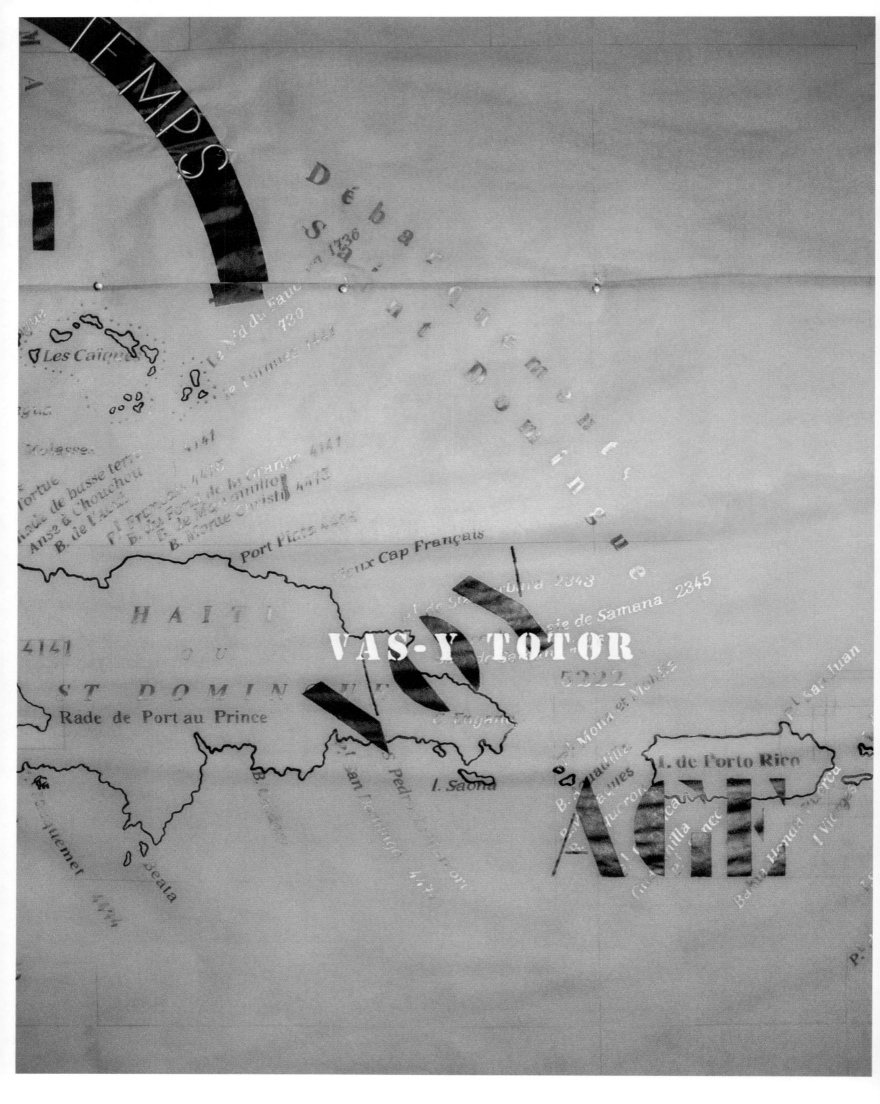

LE CORBUSIER: MURAL AT THE ENTRANCE

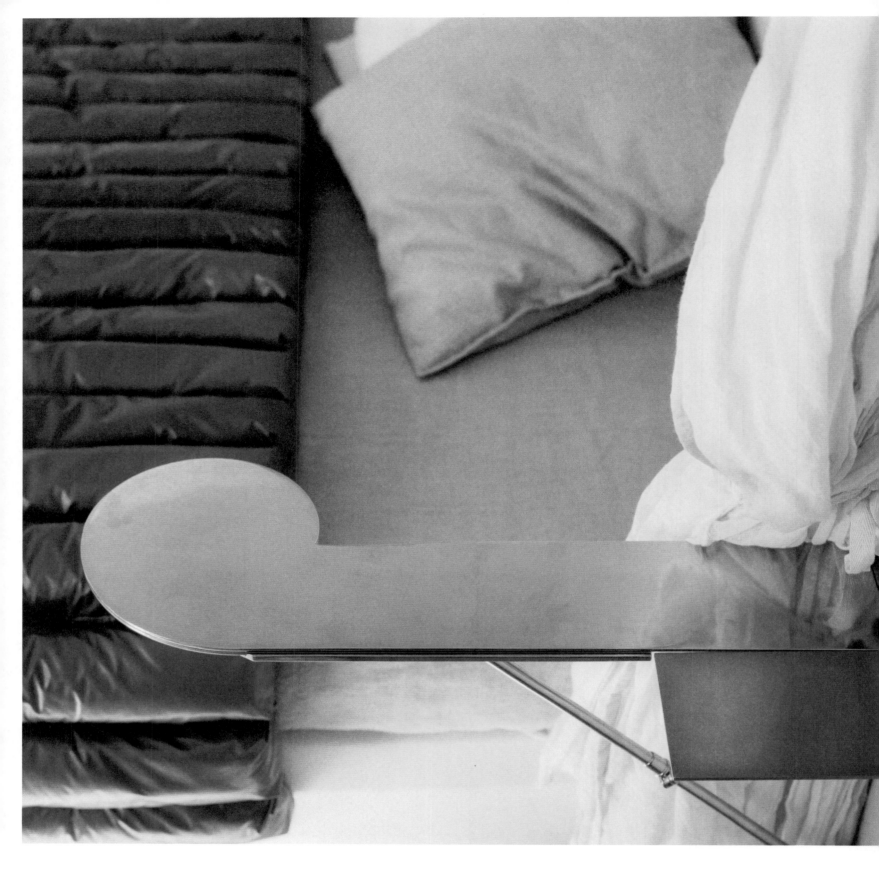

DEFENSE
DE
RIRE

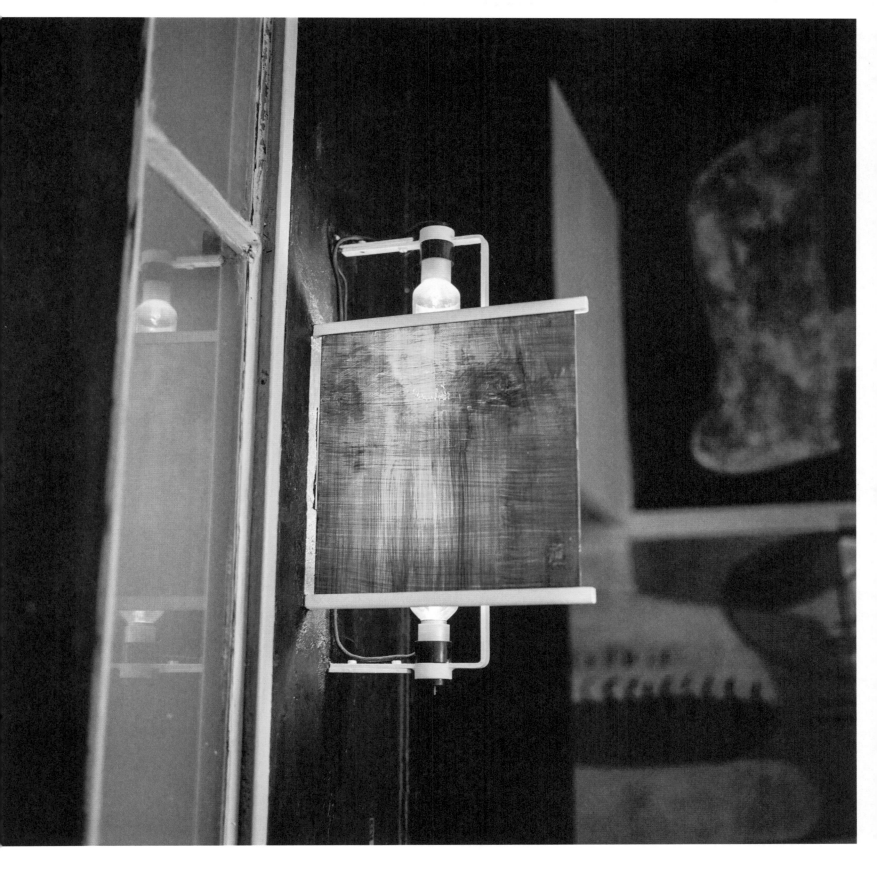

Y.
S.
L.
PIERRE BERGÉ
VILLA OASIS
JARDIN MAJORELLE
MARRAKECH 2018
—364—

HALARD

OBJECTS

+

COLLECTION

+

ARLES

+

2018

MY MASK COLLECTION

ANDRES SERRANO IN THE KITCHEN

BULL PAINTING BY MY FRIEND BARCELÓ

MY FRAMED PHOTO OF JULIAN SCHNABEL'S STUDIO

PIRANESI: JAIL ENGRAVING

MY PHOTO OF MORANDI'S ATELIER

MY PORTRAIT BY ANH DUONG

PICASSO'S HAND BY BRASSAÏ

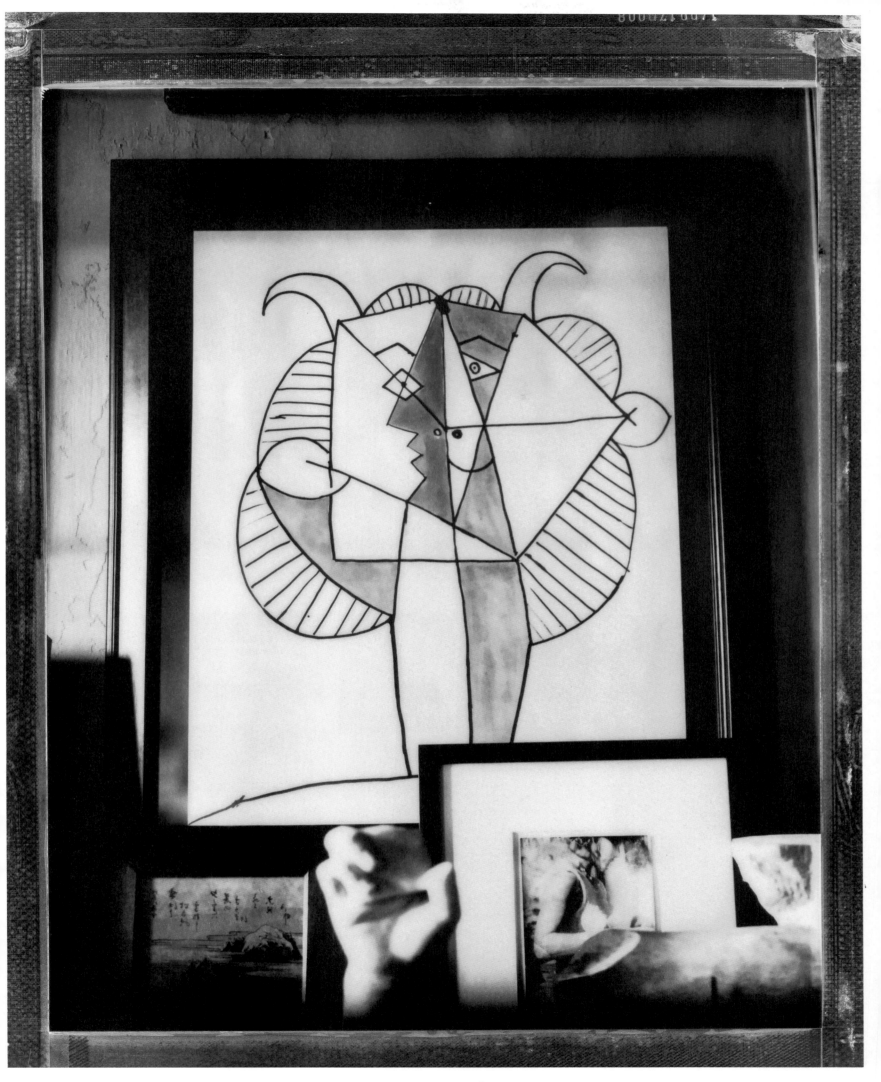

PICASSO LITHOGRAPH AND A TICHÝ PHOTO

THE GIACOMETTI PLASTER LAMP IN THE BEDROOM

MORANDI

STUDIO
GRIZZANA
BOLOGNA 2017

BEDROOM OF MORANDI'S SISTER

PORTRAIT OF GIORGIO MORANDI

CONVERSATION BETWEEN BICE CURIGER AND FRANÇOIS HALARD

ZURICH, SPRING 2019

"I'm like a water diviner.
I pick up my
camera and let myself
be guided."

Bice Curiger
Let's begin with a general
question: what's the subject
of this book?

François Halard
The book is about
artists and photography. I am
looking to establish new
relationships between them.
I'm not just photographing the
studios and homes of
artists, I want to appropriate
these interiors and interpret
them through the medium of
photography.

BC   I think of you as a
photographer of the invisible.
Not in an esoteric sense—
you're not trying to capture
a person's aura or halo
of colored light and then
interpret it. But you do show
us a part of reality that
speaks about what is not
visible in the photograph.

FH   I have often been
asked why I photograph the
interiors of dead artists.
To me, it feels like they are
still there. When I spent
two days alone in Giorgio
Morandi's studio, I really had
the impression that he was
there, that he was with me.

I tried to take photographs
that were an homage
both to his work, and to
the series of photographs
taken by Luigi Ghirri of
Morandi's two home studios
in 1989/90. I can only
translate things I love.

BC   Your perspective is
so different from the usual
style of interior design
photography. While those can
often feel like an inventory,
or even a collection of
trophies, your photographs
focus on the atmosphere and
your own presence. It seems
as if the space is talking
to you, that all the visual
signs are talking to you, that
there is a silent dialogue
going on.

FH   There's a difference
between my personal work
and a magazine article—
when you work for yourself,
you are not obligated to
give an accounting of the
space to someone else,
to give a factual description
or an "objective" representation
of that space. You are
free to say: "If I only want
to photograph one part of
a table, that's my choice."

BC   And in fact, one of the
photographs in your book
only shows a part of a table
whereas in an interior

design magazine, you would have had to show the entire piece. In another image, your eye lingers on a hallway that others might not even have looked at—and then we realize that there is so much more: a small door opens onto a cupboard painted in divine colors. This detail captures our attention and is more revealing than anything else.

FH   You sometimes can convey more through a detail, by showing just a little, by suggesting, than by photographing something in its entirety.

BC   The personal tone of your photographs is a truly artistic tone. Your sensitivity as a photographer echoes that of the artist (or collector) whose studio or apartment you are documenting for posterity. You are adding your vision to theirs.

FH   Exactly. I am lucky enough to do the kind of work that involves looking at works of art and spaces that inspire me, that I can then appropriate, so to speak, by incorporating them into my own world.
     A quick word about my childhood: I was born paralyzed on one side, so for a long

time I had difficulties with language. Most of the time I was alone in my room. The rare contacts I had with the outside world were through books, photographs and paintings. And yet, the enclosed space of my room became a space of liberation from the moment I began photographing it with my father's camera. That was how I opened myself up to the world. By photographing an object I liked that I wanted to add to my little collection, by photographing a place that made me dream, I could make it mine. I could not have taken the photographs I take today had I not experienced that period of introspection.

BC   Which brings me to Arles, your chosen city. Many houses in Arles have remarkable façades that you can't see because the streets are so narrow. And then one day, walking down a small street you walked down hundreds of times, you look up—and there in front of you is a stunning façade! It's interesting that you feel so at home in Arles…

FH   It's because of its secret side. I like secrets. I try to lead an anachronistic life in Arles. I enjoy being alone at home or in my studio. I'm like a bubble within another bubble, a little circle inside a larger one…

BC   Let's look at the book more closely. There is a beautiful narrative in the sequence of the series: one thing leads to another.

FH   We worked very hard on the selection and layout. This is my fifth book collaboration with Beda Achermann, the art director from Zurich. We began with nearly fifty stories, and each one was comprised of nearly fifty photographs. The pile of photocopies was almost one meter high! We reduced, reduced to the max, to achieve the strongest visual and narrative intensity. The advantage of doing this with Beda is that he is already very familiar with my work, and each time, he tries to push my personal vision even further. He forces me to be even more abstract, more radical. To make no concessions. Working together is wonderful.

BC   The book begins with what looks like pages from a scrapbook…

FH   For many years, I wrote and glued things in notebooks so that I would not forget. I don't like using a computer *[he mimics the gesture of typing with one finger]*, so if I want to remember something, I need to write it down. The result is a kind of collage, an unsophisticated to-do list. The pages reproduced here deal mostly with Italian topics. It wasn't premeditated, but Italy has always had a very strong influence on me. For obvious visual reasons: the architecture, the gardens, the sea… Arles is the most Italian, the most Roman city in France. It's where I discovered antiquity—and how it can be modern. And indeed, the works of Cy Twombly, or Umberto Eco, show that the themes of Italian art are incredibly modern. I shot my first personal photographs when I was sixteen, in the Giardino Giusti, an Italian garden near Verona. That's when I discovered that photographing something I like gave me a great sense of peace. It allows me to concentrate, to enter an almost meditative state of mind.

BC   I especially like the moment when the garden appears in the book's narrative. Before that, we are mostly looking at decay, faded colors, the patina of time—in short, we are in suspended time. And suddenly, the immediacy of the moment is upon us; life, fragile but bursting with colored petals…

FH   Dries Van Noten is obsessed with his garden. For him, it's almost his most important work. Photographing these flowers at their short-lived peak, made me think of fabrics that a stylist drapes over his models. My book is also a tribute to famous people who are obsessive in their taste—noted figures like Eileen Gray, Dominique de Menil or Yves Saint Laurent and Pierre Bergé…

BC   In your photographs of Dominique de Menil's and Louise Bourgeois's homes, taken well after their deaths, we can still feel the presence of these "obsessive" women. Louise Bourgeois, for example, is "represented" in a drawing and on the cover of a videotape tucked in a corner…

FH   My photographs are filled with those kinds of references. In Louise Bourgeois's studio, I photographed the cover of a book entitled "Women Artists"

featuring a portrait of a young Muscovite woman wearing a Greek costume, painted by Élizabeth Louise Vigée Le Brun, another pioneer of the art world. I also included the detail of a horizontal line of nails and hooks on a door, emphasizing the shape of a cross. This references the spiritual dimension of Louise Bourgeois's art, and its lasting relevance.

BC   In the book, you often shift from an opulent décor to its opposite, to something barren, decayed, not decorative but filled with meaning.

FH   It's difficult to make something other than decorative with photographs of decorative art. That's the real trick for me. How to use a decorative art space to lead the viewer toward something else. Sometimes, showing a personal detail, something that is not staged, can reveal a lot about an artist. At that point it's no longer a frozen photograph of an interior, but can become a narrative…

BC   You work on intuition…

FH   On intuition, yes, but it's reinforced by the deep understanding that I have about the work of Bourgeois, Philip Johnson, Charles James... When I walk into the space of an artist whose work I have thought about for a long time, all the knowledge I've acquired over time comes into play. Instead of keeping my distance, for fear of misunderstanding something sacred because it is unknown, I dive head first into the subject matter, without a second thought. I'm like a water diviner. I pick up my camera and let myself be guided.

BC   You have captured the audacity of these interiors, of their layout, in the way you photograph them. The series on the de Menil home is startling in the way you play with the light and its reflection. Are we inside? Outside? A very simple and yet very refined piece of furniture like the large mustard color heptagonal ottoman will become a symbol. It almost functions like a cog at the center of a welcoming space that invites one to linger.

FH   This double page reveals many things. It was a bold move to combine Philip Johnson's architecture with Charles James's interior design. Collectors often live in similar spaces, with the same paintings hung in the same way by the same interior designers. In this instance, Dominique de Menil did something wild: she asked James to do the interior design of a Johnson house when she knew very well that they would not see eye to eye! It's important to show the risk involved. My friend Miquel Barceló is also partial to these kinds of marriages. He hung a Picasso directly over his own drawings on the wall. And he placed an Ettore Sottsass piece of furniture against a rough surface that was never repainted. His collection ranges from Tintoretto to Warhol...

BC   When I curated the Venice Biennale in 2011, I included three large Tintoretto paintings to underscore the slightly absurd and artificial separation between the world of the old masters and contemporary art. Every artist has a relationship with art history, no artist works in a vacuum. But the public often sees only a compartmentalized presentation. Today's art allows us to look at yesterday's art from a new perspective.

Let's take a closer look at one of the artists featured in a series in your book: Ugo Rondinone, whose large-scale drawings of forests reflect his strong connection with those of the old masters. As a curator, he exhibited many artists whose works had unjustly remained in the shadows. Another example: so many books about Morandi speak of his ascetic lifestyle, but the photographs that you, as an artist, have taken of his house in the countryside of Bologna reveal very concrete aspects of that intentional austerity. Those two beds, with the cross in between, the armoire with the suitcases…

FH   Morandi lived an excessively austere existence, almost like a priest, with his two sisters. The only freedom he allowed himself was in his paintings. His home in Grizzana has no distinguishable characteristics, it's like any other. But when he recreates it in a painting, his whole personality comes to life on the canvas. Sensuality doesn't exist in reality. It is born in the painter's eye. I tried to show both, the banality of the concrete and the poetry of the imaginary. To highlight the monochromatic feeling,

I softened the colors of certain shots in postproduction.

BC   You have an eye for surfaces. The chipped and worn patina of Morandi's old metal pitcher, for instance. You can't see that in his paintings. But you see it in your photograph, which shows that this object exists in separate reality from painting—photography (which is another form of painting)… And your series on Marcante Testa, the new interior design studio in Turin. The way you frame the line of a piece of furniture to make it stand out… immediately confirms your appreciation for refined craftsmanship.

FH   I was thinking of Gio Ponti when I shot those photographs. The same artistic metalworkers who once worked for him, work today for Andrea Marcante and Adelaide Testa. It's my tribute to a tradition from the 1970s. Seamless soldering is extremely difficult. For me, it's as beautiful a craft as traditional French marquetry.

BC   Some of these photos come close to abstraction because you are standing so near the surface of the objects. The same applies to your series on Eileen Gray's Villa E-1027.

FH The most beautiful photographs of that mythic house were taken during the 1930s. Today, the soul of the period is missing. The best way to recapture that spirit is to take close-up shots—and reach a kind of abstraction. I dreamed of photographing the Villa E-1027 ever since I was a child. Things happen in their time, you just have to wait.

BC Now another story, about the Glasgow School of Art.

FH That mythic building, by Charles Rennie Mackintosh, probably the most beautiful Art and Crafts structure ever built, had just sustained very serious damage from a fire. I barely had an hour and half to visit the construction site. The photographs I took on the fly feel like stolen shots. And when I wanted to show them in 2018... a second fire destroyed everything! It felt like destiny, an unavoidable stroke of fate!

BC You also did a book on New York photographer Saul Leiter...

FH ... though 1,500 copies were printed, you can't find it anywhere. We both lived on the same street in the East Village, but we didn't know each other. One day, my friend Suzanne Demisch called: "I just bought the apartment of my next-door neighbor, Saul Leiter. Do you want to come by and take some photographs?" I grabbed my cameras and ran over... It was as if he had just gone out to do an errand. The smell of developer was still in the air. All those intimate photographs of the street—Saul Leiter had taken them from those very windows. I immediately shot what he could see from there. It was like being inside his head. When I get to do things like that, I'm in ecstasy. It's very very intense.

BC Intensity is something you look for...

FH Yes! I need things to vibrate!!

BC Finally, can you talk about the series on your house and your objects?

FH I bought this house because it reminded me of Cy Twombly's Bassano

home in Teverina, north of Rome. When you're under that Italian spell, it never lets you go! I wasn't even thirty then, and spent many years restoring it.
I didn't have any money, so I slept in a bed right in the middle of the rubble.
Back then, it looked more like the stark and punk interiors of Rick Owens than the town house overflowing with art objects that we see on the photographs.
But—alas—I can't resist things that tell a story, so the house quickly filled up.
A gift from Miquel [Barceló] here, something from Julian [Schnabel] there... I've had many houses and at one point everything was shipped back to Arles, so many items remained there because I had nowhere else to put them!

BC   What was your approach when you photographed this series?

FH   In 1935, Walker Evans was commissioned to put together a portfolio for MoMA's "African Negro Art" exhibition. He created a kind of repertoire of nearly five hundred African works shot in 20×25 cm format against an almost gray background.

I wanted to honor this work. My African masks are like my good luck charms, I take them everywhere. Some have protective qualities, others are more serious... Certain objects tell stories of past travels: my wife, Isabelle Dupuy Chavanat, likes Japanese ceramics from the 18th century, and those objects remind us of our trip to the Land of the Rising Sun. All these objects speak to one another, do things together. I photograph them with delight, with pleasure, as if they were beautiful women. They bring me the same sense of gratification.

Bice Curiger studied art history in Zurich, where she was born. She co-founded the art magazine *Parkett* in Zurich and published 101 issues over 33 years. From 1993 to 2013 she was also the curator for the Kunsthaus, Zurich's beaux-arts museum. She was the head curator of the 54th Venice Biennale in 2011. Two years later, Curiger was appointed Artistic Director of the Fondation Vincent van Gogh in Arles.

LOVE

ART
ARTIST
ARCHITECTURE

ACKNOWLEDGMENTS.

BEDA ACHERMANN / MIQUEL BARCELÓ /
ZOE BEDEAUX / ISOLDE BERGER / HÉLÈNE BERGAZ,
NOEMI BONAZZI / HAMISH BOWLES /
MARIE FRANCE BOYER / MIRANDA BROOKS /
ALEXANDRA & JAMES BROWN / MARKUS BUCHER /
ROSE CHALALAI SINGH / ÉDITION CONDÉ NAST /
MADISON COX / BICE CURIGER / ISABELLE DUPUY
CHAVANAT / TOM DELEVAN / SUZANNE DEMISCH /
EASTON FOUNDATION / EDWARD ENNINFUL /
MARGIT ERB / YVES GERTEIS / THE GILARDI
FAMILY / ANTONY GORMLEY / JERRY GOROVOY /
OSCAR HUMPHRIES / MARC JACOBS / LENNY KRAVITZ /
YVON LAMBERT / MICHÈLE LAMY AND RICK OWENS /
PATRICK LI / SUNGHEE LEE / SAUL LEITER FOUNDATION /
CAI LUNN / MARTIN LUQUE / JARDIN MAJORELLE /
ANDREA MARCANTE / ~~MENIL~~ ~~MENIL~~ MENIL COLLECTION
ÉRIC MÉZIL / CHARLES MIERS /
IRINA HOVMYGA / CLARA MURRAY / DUNG NGO /
VICKEN ~~PARSONS~~ PARSONS / JENNIFER PASTORE /
STEVEN PRANICA / PROCESSUS LAB / SIR JOHN
RICHARDSON / UGO RONDINONE / DAVID SEBBAH
ANDRES SERRANO / CORNELIUS TITTEL / PETER
UNTERTHURNER / DRIES VAN NOTEN AND PATRICK
VANGHELUWE / NADIA VELLAM / ANNA WINTOUR /
MARC ZITZMANN.

First published in the United States of America
in 2019 by Rizzoli International Publications, Inc
300 Park Avenue South
New York, NY 10010

Concept and editing: Beda Achermann

Publisher: Charles Miers
Editor: Dung Ngo
Design: Studio Achermann
Production Manager: Studio Achermann & Alyn Evans
Color Separation: Maxcolor, D-10997 Berlin
Managing Editor: Lynn Scrabis

Printed in Italy by OGM SPA, Padua

2024 2025 2026 / 10 9 8 7 6 5 4

ISBN: 978-0-8478-6565-9
Library of Congress Control Number: 2019944345

Visit us online:
Facebook: com/Rizzolinewyork
Twitter: @Rizzoli_books
Instagram.com/Rizzolibooks
Pinterest.com/Rizzolibooks
Youtube.com/user/ ~~~~~ Rizzoli NY
Issuu.com/Rizzoli

Planche VII

LE MERCURE DE FRANCE

H. Guttenberg.   D'après Lavreince.

François Halard

ITALY

I WAS 16 WHEN I FIRST AND.

~~WENT TO ITALY. I~~ MAKE
TOOK ~~SOME~~ PICTURES OK
~~PHOT~~

"Giardino Giusti" an Italian
Renaissance Garden Near
VERONA" — It was the
beginning of a collection of
~~places~~, gardens, Ruins Houses
and ~~architecture~~.
artist....

My Italian "Grand Tour"

From cy twombly To Morandi
~~studio~~ — From capri To Sicily.
— ~~Romana Malaparte~~

I am showing my most
. PLACES/ Precious Polaroid From 1984 To
Taken
2017

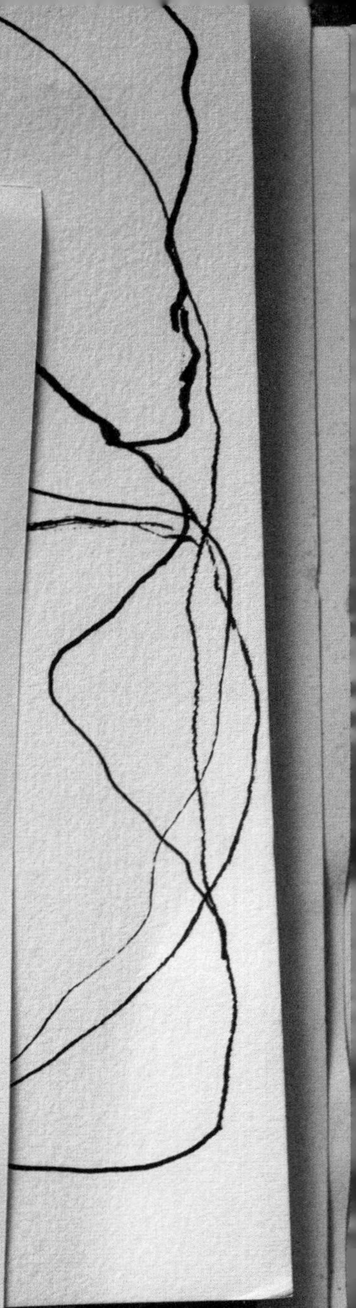

Palazzo Conservatori - Testa di Amazzone

LEMON

LES ROIS MAGES

DEMPSEY
+
CARROLL (.COM)

STATIONARY ENGRAVERS
SINCE 1878

877.750.1878

212.750.6055

CORRESPOND[ENCE]

EGYPTIAN

—

UTILSER J

JINCENT +

POLAROID I

+ PIERRE BE

МS MARIE-PAULE PELLE   ...ЛИНГРАД ГОСТИНИЦА ЕВРОПЕЙСКАЯ К±216   MR FRANCOIS HALARD

DAR ES
JARDIN MA
MARRA
MAR

МЕЖДУНАРОДНАЯ

МИНИСТЕРСТВО СВЯЗИ СССР   ТЕЛЕГРАММА

Бланк № 684 ✳

ПЕРЕДАЧА:

Адрес

TM8627 VIA ITT ZP03631700
SULK CO UIPW 051
NEW YORK NY 51/48 05 1254

MR. FRANCOIS HALARD
MS. MARIE-PAULE PELLE
HOTEL EUROPE SKAIA ROOM 216
LENINGRAD.

00 020

DEAR FRANCOIS,
YOUR PHOTTOGRAPHS ARE WONDERFUL. EVERYONE HERE ADMIRES
THEM. WE ARE THRILLED. AND, DEAR MARIE-PAULE, INFINITE
THANKS FOR YOUR HELP. WE HAVE A REMARKABLE SERIES OF
PAGES.
GRACE MIRABELLA AND ALEXANDER LIBERMAN
420785A VORK UI

VILLA OASIS
JARDIN MAJORELLE
MARRAKECH
MAROC

ALTRA VEDUTA DEL MEDESIMO

ALTRA VEDUTA DEL MEDESIMO

QUEEN PLEASURE

MARIE ANTOINETTE